the SELF
ESTEEM
SURVIVAL GUIDE

BECOMING YOUR AUTHENTIC SELF

the SELF ESTEEM

SURVIVAL GUIDE

The River Within Me

INTHIRANI ARUL

TATE PUBLISHING
AND ENTERPRISES, LLC

Published by Tate Publishing & Enterprises, LLC
127 E. Trade Center Terrace | Mustang, Oklahoma 73064 USA
1.888.361.9473 | www.tatepublishing.com

Tate Publishing is committed to excellence in the publishing industry. The company reflects the philosophy established by the founders, based on Psalm 68:11,
"The Lord gave the word and great was the company of those who published it."

Published in the United States of America

ISBN: 978-1-63418-111-2
1. Biography & Autobiography / Personal Memoirs
2. Self-Help / Abuse
14.11.28

This is for all the people in the world who have ever felt alone and for anyone who has struggled with their own self-worth.

Acknowledgments

To all the teachers I have had in my life who gave unconditionally of their selves and their teachings. I appreciated that they gave from their hearts and showed it through their patience and understanding towards my own personal growth.

This includes Dale Carnegie for their amazing course in public speaking and human relations, giving me the opportunity to face one of my greatest fears, which was to be in the presence of others and groups needless to say to speak-up. To Peak Potentials and their transforming courses the coaches, CEO Space, and their teachers.

To my father, sister, and son for their unconditional love and support. Special thanks to Shellie Hunt who saw between the lines and because of her this book is in inception. With gratitude to the amazing networks, teachers, and schools that my son attends and inspiring him in his learnings, who in turn keeps me inspired towards a brighter future for all.

To the human angels who gave so generously and unconditionally from their hearts to help me get through the most difficult and traumatic period of my life. I really want to thank people who volunteered their time like Sara Chang, who was there at the beginning of my writing journey with the children's stories. I also want to thank all those people who impacted my life and gave me the opportunity to learn through work and volunteer opportunities. This gave me the practice and ability to speak up for and with the amazing, elderly, and individuals with special needs I have had the privilege of volunteering with, caring for, and working with whom helped me find my voice.

Contents

Preface

The reason I have chosen to write this book was to serve others who may be in the midst of a self- esteem crisis, and I want them to know that there are ways to get you through this situation. What I have written is a true survival story. I am sharing with you my story in the hopes that you may learn from my journey and be able to apply some of the tools and some of the resources online.

I always believed that my life has a greater purpose, and the experiences were there for me to learn from. If I know what it feels like, I can have a better understanding and a way to relate with what another person may be going through as well in this similar situation.

No one will have the very same experience; but we can relate to the pain, loss, emotions, and the cycle we all go through. I know every person on this planet has been in a relationship, friendship or through fear, pain or experienced some form of loss at some point in their lives. I write this book in the hopes to inspire and help women with their own self esteem in the hopes that they too will find their voice and most importantly find that place of safety for them.

This book is about you and what you can do to get yourself out from that dark place within into that place of light with hope and the vision that you can have if you choose to. I learned in life nothing happens without taking action. Sometimes we need to take the first steps that we may fear and may make things worse for us before it gets better. That step can also set you free. Having gone through all that I experienced there were times that fear was over powering me. Sometimes in order to get past the fear I made the decision to go through it to get to the other side and to get to where I wanted to be. I hope with all my heart that this book helps with your empowerment to have the greatest life you can possibly have through the tools and decisions you choose to make. Always remember you deserve to be treated with the greatest respect and to live that greater life that you are so meant to live because you are here on purpose and for a greater purpose.

Anchored and Standing In Your Authentic Self

Regardless of our circumstances, experiences
and hurdles we may have had to cross and
overcome in our life's journey our authentic
self is the inner anchor from our learning's
that radiates our power from our true self.

I wanted to start this book out by saying no one in this world is perfect. We may want to be perfect, or there may be expectations from others for us to be perfect. We may be hard on ourselves if things don't work out the way we want them to. Words don't flow through our mouths the way we want them to, or other people perceive our words in their own ways they interpret them. Just remember as long as you know in your heart you did your best to convey your message is what counts and is the most important thing you can do for yourself. Remember who you are. Sometimes you may stumble and fall and you may forget and people may blame or make fun of you, but this is who you are. It is okay to be you because we are all created differently. No one is the same as another. This is what makes us unique. Some of us struggle with communication, and no one is perfect. Communication is a process; it is something that is learned, practiced, and is a lifelong journey of learning.

What is the authentic self? The authentic self is who we are. We all start out as our authentic self; and as things happen to us some people get jaded, some people get tainted, some people get bitter, and some people give away their power. The authentic self is about being seeded and grounded and standing in your power and embracing all the things that happened to us and are happening to us. My authentic self still has all of my experiences, all of my worst pains, knowledge and triumphs. And it's being able to assimilate all of my past and digest it and flourish to really be the totality of whom I am now. My authentic self is that part of me that has a higher purpose. It has a higher calling. It still has feeling. No one is in their authentic self and is a wacko. If someone operates from authentic self, they operate with a childlike expectant. They operate from a place of wholeness and anchored in who they are.

As an adult, how do I know what my authentic self is? My authentic self is the one that is okay with what I like and what I don't like. My authentic self looks back at my past and yet can see the lessons that are in it. I operate from a grounded, anchored place of power. Authentic self doesn't have to fight for power from anybody. Power is being in your authentic self.

Sometimes we drift away from our authentic self. As the things that happen to us show up as an inevitable occurrence we sometimes forget who our authentic self is, but yet our experiences and the things that we encounter make us who we are. When we are in our authentic self it embraces that. It doesn't fight it. It doesn't give up control, and it doesn't lose its power. It sits in authenticity.

How do we stay in our authentic self? How does our environment affect us and everything else, and how are we going to stay that way? Living out of authenticity means to be rooted in your deepest beliefs, values, and truth, and living a life that is a true reflection of them. For example say you are in a job or relationship where you feel you are required to do things not in alignment with your truth, leave it. You will still experience challenges, emotions, as well as greatness. At the same time, you will have the wisdom of your authentic self to guide you. You do more of the things that express your truth and less of the things that do not. Through clear intention and focus, you learn to hold yourself accountable.

You are willing to sacrifice any relationship, situation, or circumstance that violates your truth being your engrained beliefs and values. Dr. Phil says, "The authentic self is the you that can be found at your absolute core. It is the part of you not defined by your job, function, or role. It is the composite of all your skills, talents, and wisdom. It is all of the things that are uniquely yours and need expression, rather than what you believe you are supposed to be and do. Authentic self is who you were created to be. Fictional self is who the world has told you to be." Do you remember being authentic as a child? You are authentically yourself.

What does being authentic mean? Being authentic means finding the key to happiness and success within one's self, not within the society that they live in. You are authentic only when you think for yourself and creating your own thoughts needs and desires. When you live your life authentically, you are living the life that resonates or is in alignment with your inner being. You will not attach or associate yourself with destructive habits, relationships, or lifestyles. You will gain inner strength and let go of manipulation, power plays, cruelty, and hatred. As a result, you will find that your life is being lifted to a higher spiritual level.

Remember Who You Are

"As children we are authentically ourselves
with magical imaginations and dreams bigger
than ourselves and the universe at large and
with the belief that they will all come true."

In my lifetime, I have gone from being a child, and I was authentically myself; and as my life went on, I found there was a period of my life where I lost myself only to find myself again. I think many of us have done that in our lifetime and so I want to share a little of my story with you.

In the winter, my sister and I used to play in the snow and make snow men, snow angels, and even had snow ball fights. I was so happy and would also love looking out the window and watching the snowflakes fall and feel the comfort of being in my home through the intensity of the storms. While outside, I would open my mouth and catch and taste snowflakes on my tongue. I also loved watching hail and rain fall and listening to it on the car when out for a ride or trip and on the window when in bed at night. I remember being blown by the wind when I walked, and it would help push me along where I did not have to put much effort into walking. Instead I had to try to use my strength towards being grounded so I wouldn't get pushed as fast or as far. I loved spending time at the pond near the school. Watching frogs and tadpoles and catching them and releasing them. I love nature.

We used to play with the neighbourhood kids. We had lots of fun playing catch and hide-and-seek. I was carefree during the time we got to play outside and on our own in our huge acre yard. I played in sprinklers, sliding over wet plastic like a slide, played in a small inflatable swimming pool, raking large piles of leaves and jumping into them. I remember making and playing with water balloons. I played hopscotch and basketball. Hung out by the dike watching the roaring water and throwing rocks and trying to skip them in the river. I even helped in my mom's garden, and we would play on a tire swing. We would also pick cherries from the fruit trees and apples from the apple trees. I was talkative, fun, cheerful, and a loving person. I loved giving hugs. I looked forward to visiting friends and having visitors over.

I remember I had the cutest outfits that my mom used to sew us. I loved trying on the new outfits. Dad also surprised us by bringing us some nice clothes and special decorations, trinkets and treats from India when he had gone away We got to play for hours. No fear, laughing nonstop at times as it was contagious when my sister or mom would laugh. I would laugh until my eyes tear up and my stomach hurt. Where I didn't even know why I was laughing in the first place. In your childhood, do you remember ever laughing so hard that you lost control and didn't know why or what you were laughing about or your stomach hurt to the point it ached?

I was so full of energy and trust. So free to create and play without fear of what others thought of me. I was innocent and believed so much that I believed in fairies, Santa, witches, UFOs, Martians, monsters, leprechauns, and Easter bunnies. I believed that dreams could come true. Did you remember when you believed that dreams could come true, and what was your dream as a child? Every child dreams, I believe in their imagination, and this takes them where ever they want to go. I didn't even care what people thought of me. Do you remember when you didn't care of what people thought of you?

I even got to paint the garage myself. I used a paint brush and roller and had so much patience and wasn't worried about how it would turn out. I felt good about the accomplishment regardless of the appearance. I felt just authentic and myself during this time in my life. I think as children we are all authentically ourselves. I remember these days with fun and wonder how I got to be in the place I was in only years later.

Lost in the Forest

With each step I take I may not always be sure of
where I am heading, but all of it is a part of my path.

As a child I'd always dreamt that I'd grow up and get married, and I envisioned it to be like a fairy tale where I was so happy and treated well. Just like Cinderella who was an elegant princess and was rescued by the handsome, caring prince who treated her with so much respect and love and took care of her. They danced together, laughed together, spoke freely and openly with each other, and had fun times together and then they lived happily ever after. They were authentically happy. I always envisioned authentic happiness.

Those were the thoughts in my mind as I went to my husband-to-be's house to meet him and his family with my father, my mother, sister, and uncle and aunt for the first time. I was dressed in my aunt's sari as she had helped me put it on. At this point in my life, my mother was unable to see and was unable to help me prepare. As I looked in the mirror; all I could see was I looked like an Indian girl. After arriving at their house, I remember I hardly spoke. It was my husband–to-be's family and my father, uncle, and his wife doing most of the talking. The feelings that were going through me when I met my husband-to-be were a mixture of excitement, nervousness, anxiousness. I could feel butterflies and knots in my stomach. He appeared to be intelligent as he wore glasses and was tall and slender with a moustache. He was dressed professionally and had a nice accent when he spoke. He didn't seem to smile much, but when he did it was a beautiful smile.

Thereafter, my husband-to-be and I had the opportunity to meet before I returned to Canada. He came over to my uncle's house to pick me up. It was awkward as my father okayed me to go out with a man on my own as he was very strict around me going out with males. We went out for a meal, and I paid for it as I knew he was not working and was still finishing his first year of law school. After eating, we went to a hill with a view and sat on a bench and talked. He appeared to be unhappy as he said he really wanted to leave Malaysia and go to Canada. He even seemed tearful. Here are some of the lessons and process I went through. I could see there was a lot of pain and hurt in him. I was feeling really sorry for him and thought I could take care of him. Have you ever met anyone whose emotions affected you?

I really thought maybe he was just going through something emotionally. He didn't have a job, and maybe it was a temporary phase or mood he was in. But, overall he seems like a nice person. I didn't understand his unhappiness, yet I trusted my parents' choice.

It was several months later when my husband-to-be arrived and told me he never met anybody like me and that I was a good person. When he said that to me, it made me feel so warm and supported. I was the bread winner as my husband-to-be was a new immigrant to the country, and he felt he was starting all over again in a foreign place even though he had said he finished his high school in Eastern Canada. I started feeling I was starting to take on a lot more responsibility at this point as I was someone who learned to work hard and save money. Again, I thought it was just a phase. He was in the process of trying to finish law school. I cooked for him, bought whatever he needed as he was not working. We got all the arrangements for the wedding that was traditionally done from the male's family. There were communication issues between his family and my father, and my husband's unhappiness dealing with his culture shock. He learned he was unable to transfer his credentials here and would have to start all over. He also said I can't do labour work. I was starting to feel his lack of support and his frustration left me feeling like he really didn't care about our future. I could see through his communication with me that his family was dictating what we should or should not do. I felt my husband was listening to everything his family told him to do before communicating with me. I could feel my husband was experiencing culture shock. I, too, was feeling culture shock and was starting to feel out of place in my surroundings.

We would go to places to see sites after I would return from work. He called me fat and said, "You are not an Indian girl. You are Canadian." I felt degraded and not good enough. I could not understand how I was going to marry someone who spoke so lowly of me and did not seem to appreciate me for who I was. I became tearful and hurt from his painful words. Have you ever had a time in your life where you were criticized for who you were or your appearance?

With the wedding date now set and additional conflict between my father and his parents, there was tension. His parents were not at the wedding as dates conflicted, there were issues around travel documents, and they were unable to get to the wedding. Tension was growing. The communication breakdown amongst family members started to add heightened additional emotion.

Thoughts went through me of why I didn't want the wedding. There was tension between our parents, and in turn affected my husband-to-be and me. Also, the way my husband was talking to me and communicated his expectations of what he wanted and that I had to follow his rules. He called me fat, and I was feeling horrified that he thought of me in such an ugly way. I felt embarrassed and struggled with the idea of marrying someone who did not even like my appearance. What was even more difficult to digest was the fact he was setting rules and wanting to change me to be someone I was not. I felt confused, powerless, and was feeling controlled.

I was more worried about what others would think of me if I didn't follow through. Thoughts went through me that my husband-to-be was already here. The cost of everything was paid for, and the dates and arrangements of all those involved were scheduled. I was afraid of upsetting my father and disappointing him for all he has done. I was also feeling the pressure as I did not know what other people who knew about the wedding would think of me also. Another part of me was telling me that my husband-to-be was probably feeling just as scared as I was and that was why he was speaking the way he was. He bottled his feelings and forced me to bottle mine as he was not opening up to me. I was scared and did not know what he or his family would think of me or say or do if I did not follow through. I remember how his eyes glared at me in rage the look of hate and the disappointment of my very existence.

There are many times in our lives where we may feel cornered and struggle with decision making. Was there ever a time you felt torn, and did not know how to make your decision because of approval?

The next thing I knew I sat there on my wedding day with a pre-arranged marriage because of our cultural upbringing, and my husband was crying and said he regretted even marrying me. Have you ever wondered how you could end up at a certain point in your life at a certain time? Well, I was wondering that in my life at this very moment. At one point, I felt disgusted because I just married someone who I seemed like despised me. Emotionally I felt pain so severe that I was confused and was physically sick to my stomach. I was so horrified I could not understand what just happened.

This was not what I imagined as a little girl. Here's the deal all little girls think about it. They pretend they are walking down the aisle. Don't we? He started complaining that the girl should be living with the husband's family and not the man with the girl's family. He was verbally trying to control my entire life. His family blamed me and my family as they thought I was holding him back from studying further. When in actuality it was my husband's decision of not wanting to pursue his studies in Canada as he would have to start from the beginning. I felt I was being blamed for something I know I never did. Was there ever a time where you felt blamed for something you knew you never did? I knew he and his family were feeling resentful for not being at the wedding. I felt guilty and bad that they were not there as I could only imagine the pain when your own parents aren't at the wedding, which is one of the most important events of one's life. Do you agree that sometimes in life things don't always turn out the way we expect them to?

Lessons

At this point, I realized the importance of making sure both families attend the wedding. If I had noticed all the small signs of anger and self- sabotaging words, I may have not gone forward with the wedding. Not to worry about what others think of me if I walked away from the wedding. Anything I did and all that I did to help him financially was never good enough for him and his family. My self-esteem and my own unworthiness were reappearing. I could never do anything right. I was still accused of not helping. Things were twisted, manipulated around, and I was told I was good for nothing.

Even his mother and sister said that they regretted that they allowed him to marry me. They said right in front of my friend that I had ruined my husband's life. I was speechless, horrified, ashamed. No one, not even my family or friends ever told me I ruined anyone's life before. I could not understand their hatred towards me. I felt paralyzed and wanted to escape from their house but was so paralyzed from their anger I could not move. Another reason I was paralyzed was because I was so scared and felt guilty that I had provoked that within them. I did not know how to handle the situation. Tears started running down my cheeks. I just wanted to leave and never see them again.

Was there ever a time where you felt ganged up on by others, and were told you were not good enough and as a result felt not good enough? I could not understand how such spiritually conscious people could have so much anger and hate towards another person. Their venting could not stop, and nor could my tears and the physical aching of my heart. The tone of their voice and the anger in their faces pierced through my heart. My tears were so uncontrollable, and I cried so hard and felt so alone. Was there ever a time in your relationship where you felt so small and alone and so out of control with your emotions? With the hurtful words my self-esteem was going lower and lower, and if I had only known that 1 in 3 women in the world were going through this I might not have felt so alone. But at that moment in time, I was alone. I learned that I really was not alone and that according to statistics 1 in 3 women have experienced domestic violence in some point or in some form during their lifetime. I also learned that in 10 countries, 55% to 95% of women have never reported any type of mental or physical abuse to government shelters or police if anything.

I was humiliated repeatedly in front of friends and his family. Felt so degraded. However, a part of me knew who I was as I could not tolerate lies and the twisting and knew I was never going to be like that. I was always strong that way that no one can force me to do anything unethical or morally wrong. I always tried to create peace and defuse fighting by just listening and not always responding but would become emotional and isolate myself. I felt the less I said the less trouble I could get into, and it was less likely I could hurt anyone.

Sometimes being quiet can also be a trigger in those who want to control as they find ways to demand an answer. Have you ever felt threatened? How did you handle being in such a situation? I would find someone to speak to like a close friend or my family like my sister or father. Is there anyone you have a safe space to talk with and confide in?

I would find ways to see the more positive side of things and see that he was coming from his own pain that was a lot deeper than I could help him with. He spoke very little of his feelings as he would bottle that. If there was something he did not like that I may have done or said, he would give the silent treatment and then anger would show. I would become emotional and apologize for whatever he or his family would accuse me of.

The reason I felt I had to apologize was because I felt bad about my own self, and I believed I was at fault for hurting them. I do not like hurting anyone. If it comes across that I have hurt them, I hurt even deeper emotionally. If I asked for their forgiveness, they may accept me. I apologized because they had a complaint about me. I was trying to create peace so they would not hurt me further. I would ask in prayer for them to be more loving and to be happier and for the forgiveness of whatever I have done to be treated that way. I would ask for a better life and prayed that things would get better.

All of a sudden, I started to realize that I was too sick and tired of fighting. It was like a roller coaster ride. We would fight and then we wouldn't. Then we would fight and then we wouldn't. Then we would fight and then we wouldn't. It was just like this constant cycle that I really started to see, and I can't tell you how many times I prayed for that to stop. The fighting just grew and grew and grew, and pretty soon that fighting became the norm. Then you become callous too.

Have you ever ridden this roller coaster of ups and downs in your relationship?

What Was and What Is

After the roller coaster ride, there comes a time where it does not affect you the same way and you become used to the words and behaviors and get caught in it, and you end up not protecting yourself. You tolerate it and become part of the cycle. How did I become callous too, and what was happening to me?

When you first meet someone, they're always on their best behavior. The more you are around them, the more you notice other habits and behaviors. What habits and behaviors did you see as time passed that you did not see in your partner when you first met?

Looking back now, I realized I saw the anger and the lack of trust. In time, I saw very controlling behaviors of someone who may want to control my entire life. Whether I stood or sat, what I wore, what I ate, how I walked, how I looked, and the way my hair was worn, and whom I can or cannot speak with or see. I was judged upon everything. I felt worthless.

A part of me thought he may have an illness, depression, as I felt he was not happy with anything. Growing up, I saw how my parents stayed together even after my mother lost her sight progressively when I was young, and as a result had mental health issues. I saw behavioral cycles and the many stages she went through, and how my father stayed beside her to her very last breath. I spent most of my life taking care of her. I felt I was doing the same with him. I also felt my husband was worried I may leave him and felt he needed to make me feel ugly. I was married to him and knew something was wrong. I also felt sorry for him as I felt he was alone and didn't have anyone to turn to as he did not have many friends and his family was not around. He did tell me not to trust anyone. I thought to myself does that include him too. As a wife, I made a commitment to take care of him through the good and bad times. I was hopeful in time things would get better. He was my husband, and no one is perfect.

Are you someone who believes in your marriage vows, or is someone who is committed to a relationship? I tried to find ways for him to accept me by doing things he liked and tried changing myself so I can also feel safe from his anger and to win his approval of me. Have you ever experienced this type of control? I made a vow through marriage that I was going to make this marriage work. I tried to fix the marriage and was going to fix the marriage.

Darkness Emerges
through the Trees

Another person's behaviors can harbour
painful emotions and fear within us and
as a result we become submissive to them
and prisoners within ourselves.

When angry, he would not speak and would internalize his feelings. At times when angry, the words would shoot out. I would feel shock and at a loss for words and not know how to react and would become sensitive, tearful, emotional, helpless as I knew there was nothing I could say or do to have him hear me. I also feared of what he would do next. He smoked more cigarettes than usual. He would still smoke with me in the car even when I would ask if he would smoke away from me. I felt he had no respect for my feelings and needs.

When I looked into his eyes, I could see a glazed look of anger. He had the windows slightly rolled down. He took out his cigarette from the package and tapped it on the box before he lit it. The car was in motion. I could see the smoke blown out from his mouth and the smell of suffocating air I was forced to breath. I would look at him and say, "Could you please stop the car and smoke outside because I am having trouble breathing with all this smoke, and please roll the window down." Here I was sitting with him while he was smoking in the car and not hearing my feelings about his smoking. I was thinking to myself I was supposed to work this marriage out as I was his wife and I made a vow to take care of him.

I would roll my window down, and he continued to drive even slightly faster when I would speak my thoughts. I worried for our safety and the safety of those around us. I didn't want to distract his driving further by angering him. I could also feel and see the anger through his nonverbal communication and the movement of the car.

Was there ever a time in your life where you felt that you had no control and feared your safety and or the safety of others?

There were days he would go out to a bar and come home driving after drinking. Anything I said, he did not hear. I was scared to go out for meals in restaurants or special dinner outings as I feared his drinking and driving home. I feared his safety and mine. Sometimes his anger turned to rage where he was not himself and was solely acting out of his anger. Nothing anyone says or does can impact him. It only created more anger. Accumulation is like a pressure cooker where it will explode if tampered with. I could not wear what I wanted. He would comment on whom I was trying to impress by dressing up. He would then tell me I dressed like a slob. He would hold my nose up and say I look like a pig. This in turn left me feeling so much fear and despair. I felt hopeless. I didn't know who to turn to, who to talk with, as I felt no one could understand. He wouldn't let me visit my friends. My friends saw my pain. He would make me feel guilty as he would say, "You should spend time with me, instead you want to go out with your friends." It was only once in a while that I would want to go out. However, it was okay for him to go out with his friends.

Have you ever been around someone who wanted to control your every move and would do anything to dampen your spirit for control?

My husband would even try to separate me from my family after we moved. He would say when a girl marries, she is to take care of the husbands family not her own. He would yell at me if I would visit them, as well as when I called them or my father called me. He would question me and ask what they wanted. I felt isolated like I was confined. Were you ever questioned for speaking with someone? Were you ever told not to see your family or talk with them, and if you did you would get yelled at or even physically assaulted for it?

I felt like a prisoner in my own marriage and his home as he said. He said I was renting in his family's home. He asked me to pay rent, which I did, and I even paid for the bills. He would tell his family that I did not help him with anything, and they believed him. He was very manipulative and twisted things. I could not trust him, and nor could I believe him or his family. I felt so used.

I asked God, "Why is this happening to me? What are you telling me and why did my husband hate me this much?" I also knew his family despised me too, and he was acting in response to their anger too. I felt every time he spoke with his family, his anger escalated towards me.

5

Is It Me?

"As humans sometimes we become trapped in
our own emotional rollercoaster of a cycle and
question ourselves by asking is it me and in order
for us to free ourselves we must be consciously
aware and recognize the stages we are at."

At this point I asked myself if I am the reason he talks
to me and treats me the way he does. I felt I was the
one causing his anger by the way I may be wording myself.
The way I look, dress, or just because I exist in his presence.
He did say stop crying when I would. Even when I could
not stop, he would yell at me to stop. I could not control my
emotions and tears at times as it was so deep and hurtful the
things he would say and do. Am I not good enough?

He and his family said they regretted having married me to him. I could not stand my own existence or his. I just wished I was no longer in existence, and if I could just vanish and be away from all this pain. I felt I was triggering his behaviors and actions and pushing him towards finding another relationship. He was always eyeing girls and would catcall and bring them to my attention and compare their beauty to me.

When he called me fat, all I could flash on was being in school and how a boy called me Miss America and how other boys teased me for my appearance and now I am being called fat by my own husband and being told I was ugly. I was quiet and would not react to them, so they continued to bully me. Internally, I was feeling ripped apart and was in so much emotional pain. I did not have very many friends. My self-esteem, suffered as I felt not good enough that, I was ugly and was feeling rejected and felt this need to compare myself to others and felt that I could not make anyone happy, even my own husband. I felt I was in a very dark place and could not escape. I was so emotional and did not have the energy or desire to do anything. Was there ever a time you felt exhausted from just being in existence?

I tried to change myself to meet his expectations by dressing in more traditional Indian clothes, cooked and ate vegetarian as he was from a vegetarian family. I started watching more Indian movies. I disliked myself. Was there ever a time in your relationship that you blamed yourself? When we question ourselves is it me we go through a cycle.

Self-Cycle of Breakthrough

I went through the cycle of "is it me?" A cycle is like a life repetition it's something that is a series of events that can be repeated in time or in sequence. Some of this cycle we may identify right away. Some of it we may not. Knowing that we're engaged in it is the key. It's the answer.

In the Businessdictionary.com the definition of a cycle is "A periodic repetitive sequence of events in a process that plays out over time (such as a life cycle) or keeps on going indefinitely. (Such as a life cycle) 2. periodic, repetitive fluctuations from a constant average (mean) or trend line in a time series data observed over an extended period (typically more than one year). Cycles within a year are called seasonal patterns or variations. 3. Single execution of a complete set of operations in a process, from beginning to end."

There is a cycle of what we go through emotionally. I went through the cycle of "is it me?" As a matter of fact, I went through much more cycles than that. They say that a cycle is a periodic repetitive sequence of events in a process that plays out over time—over a period of a life cycle. But, I do know that it's typical or the same where we just keep circling around, and it really never changes. It's a ride of emotions consisting of the following feelings that we go through. It can be shock, denial, numbness, bargaining, hope fear or anger that are present. It can also stem from the same situation or relationship; and even though it's part of sickness, there are times we get trapped.

Even though all of the emotions that you are going to read below are a part of being human there are times that we get trapped in the cycle and never fully move out. The ability for us to identify where we are is a key for us to move forward in our lives. Ghosts of the past find us sometimes. If you see the cycles for what they are, you may not have to repeat the past. Many people that have been in relationships find the same kind of people to be in relationships with and they don't want the same kind of relationship. But they end up with it. There is really high statistics for that. The communication, and really the situation for what it is, can help us move on and attract something that is much more than what we are looking for the next time around.

Below you will find a more descriptive analysis of the 1-7 of the cycle stages we go through. You can move from the following stages.

1. Shock

    When in shock, your feelings get hurt. You ask yourself, "Did he really just say that?"

    When in shock you ask, "Did I hear that right?"

    You will think wow that really hurt my feelings.

    That hurt my physical body. This isn't the way it was supposed to be. Maybe I am wrong.

    One is not able to communicate or express oneself.

    You start to question one self and ask did this really happen.

How do I recognize shock?

Things you may think or say when you are in shock are:

- Oh my gosh. I don't believe this.
- They can't really mean that.

Shock is more about what is going on too.

I can't believe that Jimmy just yelled at me for spilling the cup of coffee. He can't possibly be angry for that. He cares about me and loves me and he has never yelled at me before.

What can we do to recognize and jolt ourselves out when we are in shock?

If you find you are in the stage of shock there are something's that you can do to move yourself past it. Allow yourself to feel whatever you are feeling without judgement. You connecting to others will help you heal. Avoid spending too much time alone. Don't isolate yourself. Reach out and ask yourself and get support. Talk about your feelings. Participate in social activities. Do some volunteer work. Helping others is a great way to challenge the sense of helplessness of shock. You can reclaim your strength and your sense of power by comforting or helping others. In this case, you are focusing outside of yourself onto someone else. Stick to a daily routine like regular times for waking, sleeping, eating, working or even regular exercise.

Find activities that keep your mind occupied. Allow yourself to feel what you feel when you feel it. You can go out and have dinner somewhere or sit in a park, and you start looking at how other people talk and engage in a healthy way. This is one way you can have a clean and healthy perspective of communication, respect, and exchange with people.

2. Numb

When in the numb stage, you have no feeling and empty thoughts. You can't think. You become frozen, and you can't move or feel anything.

The person is not able to communicate and express oneself.

You are emotionally removed from the situation. I am numbing myself because I don't get hurt.

You're emotionless. Not there. You may have trouble concentrating. You have no feelings. You have empty thoughts.

You become numb once your feelings get hurt several times.

You really don't know what to say. You may have nothing to say.

You are expressionless and have no feelings. You are not aware of your surroundings who, or what is around you. I can't make decisions when I am numb.

The following is what is most often heard when someone is numb.

When they are numb they are compliant.

They say okay.

Usually when they are asked, "How are you?" they respond, "Fine."

When asked, "Would you like to do that?" They respond, "That's fine."

They are just flat lying emotionally.

Jimmy says, "Can you dress in nicer clothes?"

Person responds, "Okay, what do you want me to wear?"

Jimmy may ask, "What do you want to eat?" Joanne responds by saying, "Anything."

When asked, "Where do you want to go?" The response is, "Anywhere you want to go to."

What can you do if you recognize you are numb? How could you break numb?

If you find that you have just turned numb and you can't feel your emotion because of some reason, you are protecting yourself. Well there are things that could assist you and reclaiming your feeling. One of the counter measures for numb is laughter as it breaks numbness. You may choose to be with and go out with your friends and laugh—being outside of everything and have a real laugh. To be in the moment to fully feel present is another way to counter act the blockage of the feeling of numbness.

You could go work out. You could go watch a girl movie like a drama or a romantic comedy. You could hang out with your girlfriends and laugh. If you have a child, tickle that child and play and laugh and hear that child's belly roar as they laugh. It breaks the block of numbness. Another way to get out of numb is to cry, to allow yourself to feel the pain. Just allow yourself to feel. The ultimate power and the enlightenment of a human being are to allow themselves to fully feel the engagement of life.

3. Denial

Denial is disbelief and not wanting to believe there is a problem. You refuse to acknowledge that an event has occurred. You do things as a routine without thinking of consequences, dangers or severity of possible consequences. Some of the things you may have thought, experienced, heard or said to yourself are listed below.

They really didn't mean it.

It happens again. You believe it can be fixed. One does not think of consequences of an action taken. Person has an affair and does not think about pregnancy or sexually transmitted diseases. It's not possible that he just hurt me.

He didn't mean it. It's not possible that happened and they continue doing the same routine.

It's okay they didn't mean what they just said. Or they didn't mean what they just did.

Disbelief, not wanting to believe there is a problem. It happens again.

You believe I can fix it.

When someone is in denial they can make excuses.

They make excuses to themselves and for others. You do things as a routine. You follow your normal routine without thinking of consequences.

Maybe they think they didn't make excuses like they didn't mean it. It's a once in a time thing.

Many excuses are made for bizarre behavior.

You do things in a routine without thinking of dangerous severity of possible consequences.

Denial enables the dysfunctional game to go on and it enables dysfunction.

A million excuses get made. You believe in these excuses.

Well he just didn't mean it. He just did this.

Another excuse may be if I was different and I just wasn't this way. Excuses can go both ways in denial.

You make excuses for the person to be excused who may have perpetrated it and then you make excuses for yourself of being responsible for this happening.

I couldn't do that because...

He couldn't do that because...

What is most often heard in denial is an excuse.

It only happens because…

I only did it because…

He only did it because…

He didn't mean it. He's just angry.

Not only could denial be about what they're doing. Denial is about them putting it on you.

Jimmy didn't come home last night because he had a lot of paper work to catch up on at work. He works long hours because he loves what he does and he is so busy with a lot of responsibilities.

What can I do to get out of denial if I am in denial?

Here are some of the things that you can do to break the games of denial. You can make a positive and negative list very honestly. Recognize and look at the events that have happened without giving any excuses, just black and white facts and really look at it objectively. Listen to your honest thoughts inside your head and start making a list by writing it down if you need to look at it objectively.

Another way to move through denial is to really honestly listen and be aware of your inner voice and be aware to the point that you become acutely aware every time you make excuses. The outcome may not be positive. You become acutely aware every time you are making excuses for behavior, language or exchange for another person. Make a list of everything that has occurred for the last 30 to 60 days. Just the facts of what has happened. Not allowing the mind to make excuses for the other person's excuses.

4. Bargaining

At this stage you are questioning.

What am I doing? Is this going to work? How do I handle this situation?

Bargaining is making a deal, and it's like making a trade. You do something and get something in return.

Bargaining can also be if I just give him enough time.

If I could just give him a child, we will be happier. If I just do this then I can make him a solid family person.

If I create or just got a home the relationship would be so much different.

Then when they get a home and the relationship dynamic doesn't change because the relationship hasn't changed just the environment changed.

Be careful because it can turn into bribing if you cross the line by going too far. If for example you say something and you don't always follow through with what you say.

It is a give-and-take situation. There may be agreements and disagreements.

You can feel bad if you don't get what you want. It can work in your favor.

Bargaining can be disappointing or it can be something very agreeable.

Maybe if I could just get this. I could have that.

Joanne, you always say if I could just have enough money then it will all be perfect someday.

If we could just get this then it would all be okay and we can be happy.

Oh, I just know if Jimmy gets this new job, it'll all be okay and we'll all be happy again.

Then Jimmy gets the new job and what happens?

Jimmy goes back to his own patterns.

Maybe if he just got a new house and we are in a new environment, it will all be different.

Then the relationship goes into the new place and after a period of time it's the same.

If I just had his child, he would be kind to me and love me.

Then they go on and have this guy's baby and what happens?

The relationship stays the same and doesn't change.

If you find yourself in bargaining, this is what you can do to get out of it.

The counter measure for bargaining is to listen to yourself. For seven days, really pay attention on listening to yourself and make a conscious effort to make no excuses for behavior verbiages or anything that the other person may do. Make no excuses in your mind.

In another words if you act different, it will be different. Instead of bargaining, you can make a list of everything that you want in your life, and how you want it to be. It's not selfish to do this. It's an appropriate boundary. What you want matters.

If you didn't have to conform yourself with other people's behaviors, make a list of how you would want to be treated. Write how you would be spoken to and pay particular attention to every time you try to conform to who you really are. You try to be different than who you really are. I guess there is compromise when we allow ourselves. We have to allow ourselves to be authentic. Is my authentic self matching the situation I am in? I am not talking about the normal compromising relationship. I am talking about the complete bargaining of self of changing your authentic self to try to fit someone else's expectation. So start to be aware in your mind every time you are changing yourself to fit. If it's somebody else's fault start paying attention to it.

For example: I can give and I can take, it must be me. It wouldn't be this way if I was different. Maybe if I'm different, it'll be different. Being your authentic self and recognizing this is who I authentically am and make a list whom am I authentically in my environment. Who am I authentically in my physical world? Who am I authentically in my spiritual world? Make a list of who are you in your authenticity.

5. Hope

In this stage we believe that things can work out and will work out. We look at the good qualities and look at the potential. We wish, we pray, we try to find ways to make things work.

It is accumulation of mental willpower.

Hope means to take risks.

It has imagination. It comes from times of adversity.

With it, we remove our blinders of fear.

It is a reason for expecting a better future.

It can be a motivating force for change.

It is something you wish for or desire with the expectation that it comes true.

Remembering back when all was new and seeing the love you felt in the other person, and it can be different.

Here is an example of hope.

Well you know as soon as Jimmy gets a job, I know we'll be right back where we used to be.

It'll all be okay.

I just know we'll get over this, and you know we'll all get back to where we're all happy one day.

I can see that it's possible. Possible doesn't necessarily mean that it is going to be. You can see that the possibility is there.

Here is what you can do if you recognize you are in hope.

Hope in that kind of relationship is that they are being kind to me right now. There is hope that the situation is going to change, but really we need to look at our own dream. You can see that the possibility is there. Hope that a relationship will work out or the situation would iron itself out is one thing, but really that's concentrating on the other person. We need to concentrate on our own dream, which is to be able to dream about whatever it is you want to do on the face of this planet. Write it down. What would it be? Start dreaming your own dream. We all hope that things are going to change, but what we are really hoping is that dynamic of another person is going to change because we see glimpses or moments of possibility of something different. That means we are tied up in being codependent, and the true hope comes from your own dream to be able to dream whatever it is you want to do on the face of this planet. Yet when we're doing that, we're tied in to our happiness being completed by the other person when real hope comes from our *own* individual dreams. The hope that everything's going to be great in this possibility to that you are really being tied into another person to be happy versus your happiness comes from your own dream.

If there was no boundary of what you could do and what you could be, and how you could live what would it be?

To step into hope you need to dream. To be able to dream about whatever it is that you want to do on the face of this planet. Write it down. Would it be to be an author? Would it be to be a lawyer? Would it be to be a children's advocate? It's dreaming. Dreaming brings hope and hope brings possibility. If there were no obstacles and you were just as an individual what would you want to do, be and have? Make a list. Really expand on the list as if there were no boundaries, no obstacles. Really write a big list. If you could be anything you wanted to be, if you could have anything you wanted to have, if you could do anything you wanted to do, what would you want to do? Then pick one you are interested in and start with it by investigating and reading up on it. If it is to be a chef, then start reading about food preparations, start researching, talking with chefs or have knowledge about what you need to know to be a chef. Start reading what it is like to be a chef. Just start looking at it.

6.   Fear

When in the stage of fear, you don't know what to expect. What is going to happen? How do I deal with this?

You feel nervous; your anxiety is high, and your heart races. You feel butterflies in your stomach, or your stomach feels tight.

You lose concentration and focus. Your hands may shake.

People go to three places in fear. They either go to anger; they cry and go to sadness, freeze and do nothing and go numb, or they move through it and go to hope.

Fear and love are very close. They have butterflies in the stomach.

Their fear is "I may get hurt, or someone is going to get hurt."

You may become tearful or laugh at inappropriate times. Some people become angry.

You feel scared of the unknown.

You don't want to do something because you don't know the outcome, or you can predict the outcome. You're afraid of being alone or not being able to support yourself or your children.

Maybe he won't function without you, or he will never find another relationship. You don't feel strong and that you are not good enough. You are upsetting others. You are a constant problem.

You think no one else will love you.

You feel scared, you feel alone and that you are by yourself. Not trusting and not knowing where to turn for help or direction.

You may feel threatened for your safety or for the safety of the other person if you cannot manage your anger.

When you recognize that you are in fear here is what you can do.

No human being should have to be in a situation or a relationship where they fear for their life. Fear can give you incredible strength. If you feel your life and physical body is in danger, one of the things you can do is cautiously remove yourself from the situation.

Firstly, fear and love are two of the most powerful emotions. Fear and love are very close. Fear can be a catalyst of change. Fear can give you incredible strength. In your imagination, think of what it is you fear. Ninety percent of all things that we worry about may not come to pass. All things that we worry about may not happen. But what would life be like without living in that fear? Imagine not having that fear and having what it is that you wanted to do or have. Imagine yourself in that situation achieving or doing or having what it is you want and visualize and really be and feel it and use all your senses as if you were right there.

7. Anger

When in the stage of anger, you feel you have had enough. You want to get out. You are at the point where you feel you have over stepped your boundary.

You feel it when you are at your limit, and you can't take any more of the situation. It is built up. You don't know how else to handle the situation. You feel you can draw attention to the other person or to yourself to be heard.

You are not present. Your body becomes rigid.

It can be explosive when it builds above the limit.

Anger can be controlled by taking a deep breath and focusing on happy thoughts. Anger is restless.

People make justifications when it comes to anger.

People usually lose verbal control in anger. They will either say nothing and go into avoidance, or they will lose verbal control.

Communication becomes strained, and one may say things that are hurtful.

Jimmy you need to get yourself a job because I am not taking on all the responsibility for everything while all you do is lay around and watch TV and go out with your friends.

Jimmy if you are going to complain about my cooking tasting terrible maybe it is time you take cooking lessons.

If you find yourself in anger, here is what you can do to move yourself out of it.

Anger and fear are very closely related. You channel your anger. Anger is a very powerful emotion. Underneath it all, anger is always result of fear. Anger can also look at and recognize your strengths. Make an inventory list of your strengths that you've gained from this experience. Make a list of what you want differently in your life. When anger focuses into a positive direction, it can make a huge stand for change, not just for us, but on the face of this planet for others.

What's come out of anger are a lot of non-profit companies, a lot of things to help women, children and other people. They became activists. Out of anger you can become an activist for something that you believe in.

In conclusion, all these emotions are a part of who we are. All of these emotions are a learned response due to circumstances that we experience. All these are emotions that we have all felt at one point or another. Whenever we go into a situation of distress or uncertainty, we go into shock, numbness, denial, bargaining, hope, fear, and then anger. These are all the emotional stages we move through when confronted with a situation we do not know how to handle or are uncomfortable handling.

These emotions can be experienced for a short time or extended time depending on the situation encountered and the duration, the intensity and circumstances of that experience.

One can move from stages one through seven repeatedly until one makes a decision they had enough. They either leave the situation or resolve it with outside help or becoming aware of their own emotions and their self-talk when in them. It is through your own awareness of your emotions, your self-talk, and the stages you are in that you can make changes. Also know and be aware that sometimes we jump around these different stages and yet still live in the cycle of this game. People don't have to go through stages one through seven. People can jump around. Sometimes people go from fear to hope. Sometimes people go from fear to bargaining. Sometimes people go from shock to bargaining. Just like the cycle of grief, you could go from any one of these stages to another. It's not always going to be in a row. Sometimes these stages of one to seven you go through in a row until finally you move away from this cycle. Sometimes it's not one through seven, you could go from shock to anger to bargaining. People can revolve in the same game.

It is through awareness of your thoughts that you get the clarity of what you need to do next to feel better about yourself and the situation at hand. "Everything happens for a reason, and that reason is there to serve you," as stated by Adam Markel, the CEO of Peak Potentials. It is there to teach you a lesson of growth. It may be there to teach you to set boundaries for yourself or to teach you to be patient. It may teach you to speak up and express your thoughts and feelings. Teach you to be persistent, responsible, on time. The reason may be to learn to keep yourself safe, to trust yourself or others. Or the lesson may be to learn to accept yourself for who you are and to be confident in knowing that you are a unique being and are just as important as everyone else.

As addressed above. All these emotions are a part of who we are. And all of these emotions are a learned response pattern and in my own life—I know I have gone through this cycle in many different ways. For example I can go from denial, to anger, to numb, to bargaining and then to hope.

We all go through these cycles, and sometimes its financial reasons. An example is when I am going through a financial situation and I need to raise some money for an unexpected payment. Now I am in the middle of this. Fine, I need to figure this out. This only happened because I wasn't told about this extra amount. I'm in denial. I'm laughing. Are you kidding me? Now I am in shock. This can't be happening. What just happened here? It can't be what it is. Now I'm in fear. How am I going to come up with this? I am now numb. It's fine. I can't move. I can't think about this now. It doesn't matter. Now I am bargaining. Maybe if I can refinance a loan I can get the funds to pay the unexpected payment. Maybe if I just say no, I can just walk away from it. But then I will lose all the money I have already invested in it. I am now hopeful.

It's all going to work out. I will find a way to get the money for the payment.

I am now angry. How could this possibly happen to me. I can't come up with this money in such a short time. It's impossible. They are not being realistic. How dare they have such an expectation? What do you mean it wasn't calculated in the original calculation? Now I am in shock. What? Did I hear you right? What do you mean? Numb. Alright I have to deal with this. What can I do? Bargaining. The quicker I figure this out the fewer penalties I will have to pay. Fear. Everyday this continues the cost is increasing due to the penalty, and I can't afford that. Anger. Now I am in tears. How did I get myself into this mess? I'm never going to make another big purchase again. Hope. I'll take a deep breath and I know it will all work out. The right people will help me get the financing. At the right time it will all come together. It always does.

6

When the Waters Rise

*Adversity is inevitable. You are not
alone as we all experience it at varying
degrees at some point in our lives.*

We have all had things happen to us in our lives and we have asked this question.

"Why is this happening to me?" I don't know about you but, I sure have. There are times in our lives we all ask this question. Sometimes it's about birth. Sometimes it's about death. Sometimes it's about money, and sometimes it's about matters of the heart or breaking hearts. But I think that all human beings at some point in time have asked, "Why is this happening to me?" I want you to know you are not alone. I want to share more of my story with you.

When I was visiting in Malaysia, my husband was furious with me and struck me with his hand and hit me. I went into the bathroom and locked the door in fear that my husband would hit me again, as he was angry after speaking with his mother. I could see the frustration and anger in him, and how much they regretted having me as part of their family. I stayed in that washroom, sitting on the corner of the bathtub crying. I was so distraught as they did not like me calling my parents, as they too were visiting Malaysia at the time. They said, "You always talk with them. Did you come to Malaysia and to our house to see them and your relatives or see us?" They tried to isolate me. I just wanted to isolate myself from them too. I could hear my husband calling me to come out of the bathroom and pounding the door. I did not respond to tell him how I was. He did not deserve to know of my existence for the way he treated me.

After an hour, I could hear a ladder outside the window of the bathroom and up climbed my husband to check through the window. He asked me to open the door in an angry voice. He said, "What do you think the neighbours are going to think? You are giving us a bad name." All I wanted was some time to myself and keep myself safe.

Sometimes we need our own space to keep ourselves safe and to collect our thoughts and to calm ourselves. I finally came out of the room, and he and his family did not speak with me for some time. I had no faith in these people. I could not trust them, and how do I trust? I asked myself who am I?

Who are these people? Where did that carefree child go, and where am I? I felt I was in another world. I remember myself saying, "Why is my life here?" I didn't trust myself, and I could not trust anyone else around me. I didn't know how to help myself through the pain my own depression as I would cry. Whenever he would say something hurtful, it would trigger me to cry; I would dislike myself as I am someone who will not hurt someone else consciously. Instead, I hurt myself by internalizing the pain. Somewhere I sat and pondered why this is happening to me. I don't know how I got here.

I don't know how I got to this point. I isolated myself from creating relationships and friendships because I did not want anyone to judge me because I didn't like myself nor love myself. I could not understand my existence. I had forgotten who I was. Depression set in. I would be so fearful around his family about their anger and their lack of trust in me. They never took the time to get to know me. I would find places where I could be alone. I would drown myself out with music or funny movies.

Work was a place of escape. I would exercise to forget about my problems for a short while. Sometimes I would cry hard and land into my pillow and cry myself to sleep. People at work thought I had a cold many times and sensed I was not well. I slept very little as I would stay awake many nights worrying, in so much pain and unhappiness.

On one of my trips to his families place as we were meeting with his mother and going on a pilgrimage to the temples in India, my husband was physical and even hit me across my face in front of his mother at the New Delhi airport. His mother said to me, "You must like it when he hits you." The emotional pain was excruciating as we were in a public setting; and secondly, he had no remorse, nor did his mother; and thirdly, I did not know how much more he was capable of hurting me. Even a cousin had seen me at the airport on our return from the trip and had told one of my aunts he had seen me but did not want to approach me because he could see I was not doing well. I was emotionally drained as I had no one to speak with about my feelings. My husband had my passport and money, and I had no way of getting away from them. It was emotional torture. When I asked if they could send me back, they said if I was to go back it would give them a bad name. I even became emotionally numb. Sometimes in life we can feel there is no way to escape, and we feel trapped. Was there ever a time you felt trapped?

Looking back now, I had become so guarded emotionally at that point in my life. My authentic nature, my laughter, was not there. Negative thoughts were constantly going through me, and I cried so much my eyes would swell. I was so numb to protect myself against getting hurt. The more I went through the way he talked to me and the more I went through the way he physically was with me, I realized the more I shut down to protect myself but, in actuality I was shutting down to my life.

You are not alone. It doesn't matter if it's your social status. It doesn't matter if it's your cultural status or your age. Any of that doesn't matter. You need to know that if you're in a situation like this or anything like this you are not alone. As mentioned in chapter 3 and according to statistics, 1 in 3 women have experienced domestic violence in some point or in some form during their lifetime.

Riding the Waves

We all have our own experiences and our own perceptions of those experiences. One's own personal experience may not be seen or perceived the same way through the eyes of another.

We have all had experiences that, at times, are beyond words that are mixed with emotion with feeling with our hearts. Then again after we've all wondered why is this happening to us, we start to question our own thoughts. We start to question if we're not the ones losing it. By losing it I mean not perceiving reality correctly. We start to really wonder if is it us?

You are trying to make sense out of a mad house. You question yourself. Am I losing it, or is it really a mad house?

You start second guessing yourself sometimes by the situation. Have you ever wondered about your own sanity in the middle of a madhouse? Is our perception really reality? We start to see through distorted lenses in some way because sometimes when we're in it, we can't see it. It is about challenging experiences where you felt helpless. We've all had experiences where we've all felt helpless. Have you ever had experiences where you felt helpless? Have you ever wondered about your own sanity in the middle of a madhouse?

I know that many of us have stories, but it is very hard to be able sometimes to see what we're in and when we're in it. Let me share with you a few more of my experiences.

We had international students living in our home. My husband had returned to Malaysia two separate times to finish his second year and also the third year in law school. The first time he returned, his father was very sick with cancer and my husband was taking care of him plus studying. When I visited that time, his family seemed to really love me and appreciate me.

The second time I went back, it was a completely different story. This time when I visited, his father had passed away and his family treated me differently. They were blaming me for my husband's reluctance to study and work in Canada, as well as his unhappiness claiming I didn't help him. When in actuality, I was helping him. Meanwhile, I was paying rent to stay in his house that his family had purchased and that my husband had said he was paying down.

He rented the rooms to pay the mortgage as his brother had paid for the house in full. I also paid for the bills, phone, and even for the fridge and the furniture I had bought. He had told his family I did not help with anything. They really showed their anger towards me on this second visit. My husband would yell at me in the presence of his mother. One time that I remember really stood out was when he said, "You are no good for nothing. You don't even know how to cook, my mom is old you should be doing the work." I was in his family's house. I didn't want to do any more wrong things, and I didn't want to be in their space to anger them further. I was already uncomfortable as they had so many rules in their house. I didn't want to overstep anyone. I also know everyone has their own ways of cooking food they like. He told his family I did not know anything about the cultural ways because I had no cultural upbringing. I felt he was trying to outcast me. His mother and oldest sister said I ruined his life. I felt so humiliated and despised. When a woman has her menses she is not allowed to be on the lower part o their house which had a temple downstairs. I was forced to stay upstairs for seven days. I had to wake up and hand wash my clothes and hang them outside on the balcony of the bedroom to dry, and I had to mop the upper floor and my room each morning. My food was brought to my room. Knowing the limitations of where I was allowed to be during those seven days, I would still get yelled at for not spending time with his family or talking with them or helping them. I felt trapped as I knew I could not go down; their expectations made no sense to me. No matter what I did, I could not make them happy. I really felt the culture shock myself. I could not call my family as they would say, "You see your family so much. You have just come here for one month and can't you stay without calling them? I felt so much anger towards them for trying to separate me from my family. My greatest worry was my mother as she was someone who had a lot of medical complications, and she would always ask for me. I would worry about her. They never asked me how my mother was.

The family controlled what I wanted. I felt helpless and felt so much pain and resentment towards this family but could not express my feelings. I started to feel numb. Do you remember having challenging experiences where you felt helpless?

My husband also had a relationship with one of the students who was renting the rooms. I noticed every night, this girl was always awake and in the kitchen speaking with my husband after he returned from work. He had taken her for eye surgery and to all her appointments. Every evening I prepared a plate of food that I placed in the fridge for him to heat and eat upon returning from work. One night I woke up as I could hear a lot of laughing. As I approached the kitchen, I could see her eating off his plate with him. I questioned the both of them and went back to my room. I was feeling very hurt as I felt there was more going on between the two of them. He came into the room and slapped me and hit me really hard on my shoulder and even shook me. I broke down into tears and said, "How could you hurt me, and why is she eating off your plate with you. I don't even eat off your plate." I told him I was going to leave the following morning as it was late. That night I cried myself to sleep, and the next morning I packed my things and left. He had called me and said she was leaving and going back to Korea. He wanted me to return home. After she left, he got phone calls from her and I could hear them talking. He sounded so happy. This made me feel sick to my stomach.

Was there ever a time in your relationship where you felt betrayed or lied to, when you felt your heart was being ripped out from you or the carpet was being pulled out from under your legs?

I left again and went back to my family's house. A week passed, and I did not hear from him so I prepared food. I was thinking about him and concerned he did not eat. I took the bus as I knew his break place and the time. As I approached his bus stop from a distance, I could see another person with him. I could see his arms open wide as if he was going to give this person a hug. As I got closer I noticed it was the very same student he said had returned to Korea. I said, "I thought you went back to Korea," and my husband said she came back to visit. I was furious. I said, "How could you do this to me?" I gave him the food and left immediately. I never heard from him for at least two weeks, and nor was I going to call him. On the second week, a friend of his showed up knocking on my parent's house door. I went to look, and it was an older man. He said he was a friend of my husband's and that my husband was waiting in the car and wanted to talk with me. I refused, saying he has a girlfriend and he doesn't care about me. He said he really wants to see me and that girl is nothing to him. He spoke with a strong accent.

After he talked with me for a while, he encouraged me to meet with my husband so I went over to the car. He asked if we could go somewhere to talk and eat. I said okay. My husband had told me the girl was staying in the house for a month, and she will leave thereafter. I was still furious as she was living in the house with him. He said she does not have another place to stay. I really had a hard time understanding. Every day my husband would come and pick me up after work and would go out with me and return me to my parent's home and would try and talk to me about how much he cared about me. It was hard to trust him anymore. It was like we were dating, as they would say in Western culture. After a period of time, she did finally leave the house, and I went back on his doorstep and resumed living with him.

When you thought the relationship was over someone would try to help you work things out to bring you back together again because that's the way they think it's supposed to be. She finally did leave the house, and I returned to his house.

If we were strangers and we walked into our own situation that we've been living in or tolerated or tried to figure out or fix. Would we stay in those situations? Would we look at our friend or look at ourselves in the mirror. Another words if we were a part of our own lives and we walked in and saw this going on would we tolerate it or is it because we have become accustomed overtime being treated a certain way. How many times if we could step right beside ourselves and we didn't live in our situation and we went to our friends house and we saw how they were living would we tolerate it or what advice would we give? However, because we are in it, we become accustomed and trained to tolerate things that would be completely not tolerable.

The Reasons Why We Need to Stay in the Situation

We all look back with hindsight and wonder why did I stay in this situation? Why did I put up with what I put up with? Why did I allow what I allowed? I really wasn't sure at that moment in time. I'm sure we've all been in these places, because sometimes it's a very human place to be in. We're all in this together. I look at you and say what was I thinking? I'm not quite sure. Why did I stay in that situation? I am sure we have all asked ourselves that at different times. Sometimes because of the way we grow up and our perception, we don't want to talk about the situation.

I worried about the reputation of myself and my family's and his family's feelings. Legal expenses and complications were another concern. I don't want to hurt anyone even more. I felt sorry for him as I felt he was depressed and was dealing with culture shock. I need to be patient. I need to learn to forgive. Marriages all have their difficulties, and you need to stick through the troubled times. I believed when you marry, you marry for life until death do you part. I am a caregiver, and I have always been a caregiver. I also believed in being loyal. But I lived in fear of getting hurt further and of the unknown of what the family may do or say as they were wealthy and threatening.

If you have ever been in a place like this, what were your reasons? Why did you feel you needed to stay in the situation?

We are all creatures of habit. We all have habits that we fall into and begin to get comfortable with. Maybe you feel comfortable or you felt comfortable, and you were afraid to leave because you may be alone. Maybe you felt that no one else would love you. We are all creatures of habit, and we get very comfortable even when we are with or around somebody who may not be good for us or doesn't necessarily serve us in becoming a better person.

Habit is like a pattern or routine that you are used to doing, and you just keep doing it because it has not been acknowledged and recognized by you and comes from the subconscious place of this is the way it usually is. You usually don't need to think much as it is something you are comfortable doing or know how to do. You don't need to worry about rocking the boat or upsetting anyone or disappointing yourself because it didn't work out your way or the way the other person or people may want it to turn out. Fear comes in, and it is so much easier because nobody else might love you. You feel you are not good enough to make anyone feel happy because you can't seem to be happy yourself in your relationship. How can anybody else possibly see the good in you and love you? Therefore, we feel comfortable where we are and stay because we fear of failing and getting hurt even more.

It could be the suffering from the low self-esteem that you have forgotten that you could take care of yourself. Who would take care of you, and who would love you? Statistically, it is stated that 80% of women agree that every women has something about her that is beautiful, but they do not see their own beauty. More than half 54% of women globally agree when it comes to how they look and they're their own worst critic. If it is shown that 54% of women are their own worst critic, the last thing that is needed is for somebody to be calling you these names, reinforcing your own acceptance of self. Girls are three times more likely than boys to have a negative body image already.

Caught in the Tide

*Repeated emotional or physical turmoil through
life's experiences and within a relationship can lead
to exhaustion, which lead us to make decisions
through that troubled state of mind we are in.*

Here are some of the reasons why we feel we need to stay in the situation. You don't need to stay in the situation but you feel you can't leave. We keep telling ourselves we love them. It could be a totally dysfunctional and a very unhappy relationship, but we keep saying, "I love you." We keep remembering what they used to be like, or what we thought they used to be like. Sometimes we allow them to stay because they are a parent of our child; we have a paradigm that they are a parent of our child, and we are supposed to make it work.

Other reasons are that we don't value ourselves. When we don't value ourselves, we can't value others around us. We don't see the difference of what it is like to be treated well. We are in a cloud and are used to the way we have been treated. We become adapted to the behavior. We think they are protecting us. We think we are being taken care of. We stay because we are thinking we are protecting them as we see them as having a problem. We start thinking we can change them. We may feel sorry for them.

What caused me to look at the situation was that I was not happy and was emotional and numb from all that went on, and the thing that was going on in my mind was that I was lost and tired and didn't want to fight. I also didn't see the difference any longer as I became used to the way I was treated and thought this was the way he cared about me and protected me from the outer world. Is it safety plus security and acceptance that we feel a need to stay in the situation for?

It is having the safety, security, and learning to accept each other. If you tell the family it is going to be an issue. Why else do you stay in those situations? You care and think you have fallen in love. It becomes a routine. I have to work it out. All marriages have their problems. There obviously was something I made up in my mind that I couldn't leave. Maybe I thought it was going to get better just like we discussed in the cycles. Maybe the unknowingness of what was outside of this or maybe I just became accustomed to it.

The Gift

*Life is a school. Everyone we meet is our
teacher. Everything we experience there
is a lesson and something to learn.*

G ifts come in many different forms, and the worst things
that I have been through in my life have also turned out
to be gifts. They have turned out to be really incredible gifts.
It has taken me so long to realize that. I always believed there
was a reason for everything that happened in my life, that
there was a higher purpose for me and I had to experience the
things to authentically understand and feel what I needed to
get to where I am now. If I had realized the gifts that I would
get out of things, maybe I would not have fought them so
much. But, I gained so many things and I learned so much

about myself and what I would and wouldn't deal with. In the worst of everything, there are gifts. Sometimes living through adversity leads you to a gift.

A gift can come in the form of a life-changing event or in a form of a message spoken to you by someone, or even a strong inner feeling. A gift can come to you by someone in the form of anger. Or a gift can come to you in the form of love and compassion. A gift can be in the form of an awareness of yourself and or others. Sometimes a gift can result after a painful experience to make you more aware of your surroundings and actions.

Have you ever had an experience where things did not go the way you wanted it to? The gift in this case may be to divert you so you do not make a decision that could either bring harm or create a bigger problem for you.

I acknowledge the gifts that were given to me. It enabled me to speak up. Through the knowledge I gained from my experiences, I can now see patterns and behaviors in others. I am highly sensitive of negativity in environments and in a work environment. I advocate for respect when coworkers are being verbally or emotionally disrespectful towards me. I learned I was a people pleaser. I learned I will never advocate for another arranged marriage for myself or another person. I am very receptive of how people communicate. I am very selective in the people I choose to get close to or work with or bring into my circle of friends. I continue to work on my own personal growth. By empowering myself,

I will empower others naturally. When negativity at work got too extreme I removed myself to heal and demanded change in the environment before my return. I understand the pain when someone's partner was not truthful to them in their relationship.

I see signs of betrayal. My gift was I will only be in a committed or monogamous relationship. That's what I really want. I really want to be independent and financially independent and not solely dependent on anyone else as a partner can either leave you or pass away. I gained spiritual awareness.

What were your gift and the gifts you received from all that you experienced? Was it strength? Was it compassion? Was it kindness? Was it learning to set boundaries? Was it self-control? Was it to give unconditionally? Was it to communicate effectively? Was it how to be a good listener? Was it how to respect your body? Was it that you are creative? Was it that you needed to feel the pain to understand the pain in yourself or others? Was it that you had enough, and it is time for a change? Was it that you are not on the right path, and there is something else you should be doing? Really take a few minutes and think of each of the events in your life and what was the gift that came out of each event?

The Aftermath from the Storm and the Rising Waters

As human beings, we are sensitive to words.
They can empower us or disempower us.

Words can be so damaging. I could feel the pain in my heart. It was aching from the damaging words. It drove me into darkness, and I did not feel good enough. My own unworthiness was rearing its head within me. I felt isolated that I was not good enough. The words wounded me. I started to believe what he said about me. He said I was ugly, fat, no good for nothing. When he said this, it brought back memories from my high school years when I was teased for my appearance by a certain boy in my grade. I felt the lack of acceptance and my self-esteem was taking a beating again as here was someone who vowed to care for me that was not accepting me at this period of my life. I thought that I would not experience that disapproval again. Here once again, I was wrong.

Verbiage

Why are choices of words really important? Words can be empowering or disempowering. We as children can be formed by the words we hear and the words that we believe. We can shape a child's personality through our choice of words. We can shape a child's future with them. We can shape our own future with them. They affect what we do.

Sometimes, I don't think we realize the effects that we really have on those in our inner circle even when we say something out of anger. We affect their self-esteem we affect their ability to focus and concentrate and their ability to be carefree and damage them on a deeper emotional level. Sometimes we don't notice the verbiage, and how words are really important. We don't notice because we become used to the words and internalize the feelings or act out through similar use of verbiage through frustration and anger. We become immune to the words. We have the ability to be able to choose our words carefully. Sometimes we can have people around us that don't even realize the negativity or the positive uplift that they bring into our lives until we really step back and look at it.

I could remember the first time when somebody said I was fat and ugly. I was horrified. Well by the fifth time I heard it, I started getting numb. A year down the road, I started to believe it. Sometimes we can say things that we don't necessarily mean out of anger. We could definitely sometimes speak out of turn. But when we do say things out of anger, we sometimes hurt the feeling of others and damage their self-esteem as we internalize what we say thereafter. When you get called fat, it is horrifying. What you get used to. Words can damage and leave emotional scars. We can speak out of turn.

Why is it so important to communicate? It is important to communicate so our true thoughts and feelings can be understood. Why are the choices of words really important?

I could remember the first time I was called fat and no good for nothing. I asked myself, "Did that just happen?" I can't believe he just talked to me like that. I really started believing I could not do anything well as I would become unconfident and nervous; my hands would shake, and my concentration would diminish and the inability to accomplish something would be more over powering. Sometimes I don't think we really know the effect on the other person. When we get used to the words you become callous too. It does not affect you the same as you become used to the words and behaviors and get caught in it. You end up not protecting yourself, and it becomes the norm. You tolerate it and become part of the cycle.

How Verbiage Affected Me

The words and verbiage affected me on a deep level. It demoralized me. I felt humiliated and so small. I felt worthless and helpless, like I was a prisoner within myself. I felt unworthy, depressed, and wished that I did not exist. I did not love myself, nor could I accept that anyone else could love me either. The wound was so deep that I did not know how to heal it. I would even look in the mirror and see myself as ugly, fat, and unwanted by anyone as I could see the deformity of my my eye. Especially when I was tired, my eye would be crossed and would really be noticeable. Also one eye was smaller than the other one. Even all the moles on my face were also very obvious, and there was no way to hide it. I also struggled with my weight at times. When teased of my appearance, it made sense as those who commented on my appearance were able to see it visually and were not making up what they saw. I believed them because I could see what they were talking about. Even my husband commented on my moles, saying that too many of them looked ugly. The words took me to a dark place where my self-confidence and self-esteem suffered. I would easily become nervous and lose focus and direction and felt I could not achieve anything as no one would want to be in my presence. I lived in constant fear of others of what they would think of me even through their non-verbal communications. My anxiety level was high whenever I was around people it did not matter where

I was. I was in fear of being told how worthless I was and the affirmations of it. My heart would race as I could feel it beating fast. I would even perspire when I get on a bus and everyone would look at me, or even walking along a street. I worried what they were thinking of me. I spoke very little while in groups as I feared what people would say in response to whatever I may say as they may disagree about my opinions or thoughts. I feared more rejection.

I didn't start out this way, but again I have lost my authentic self. I am a far cry down the road from where I started.

Some people call this type of treatment brain washing, some call it mental abuse with thought reform and manipulation. I honestly had totally forgotten authentically who I was. This name of not being good enough; I believed the words. It came to the point where I came to believe the word and not listen to my heart or my soul of who I was. As a matter of fact, I didn't know who I was. I allowed the verbiage and the words to affect me. The mental abuse, coercive persuasion with thought reform is an attempt to change the thoughts of another person against their will. It's manipulation until you don't even hear your own authentic voice anymore.

What is language? Language is the verbiage that we communicate with. Why is language so important? Because it affects everything we do, we say, we think.

- Language is a very important thing. Language can really dictate how we interact with other people, and how we feel about ourselves.
- What I can do to facilitate controlling my language might be to put thought into what I am going to say before I speak.

I learned to really pay attention to the words that come out of my mouth and I hesitate for three seconds before I actually speak especially in anger. As you move forward into the future, really be aware how you speak with your children. Be aware of how you speak with children and to speak with positive words. Use words that are warm, nurturing, motivating, encouraging even when they make a mistake. Have dialogue with your children, communicate regularly and openly. Ask open questions. For example, you can ask, "How was your day? What would you do differently? What did you learn from that experience?" Thank them for sharing their thoughts and feelings with you. Acknowledge them.

Understanding Boundaries

The Boundaries of How Someone Talks to Me

Boundaries are vital to maintain our self-esteem
and our personal growth. It is through the use of
our boundaries we can become our personal best.

How Do I Get Back to Being Who I Am?
This Is What You Can Do with Your Self Talk.

We all talk to ourselves. Self- talk is that little voice that
is inside our head. The self- talk is what plays in our
heads. Those are the tapes inside our mind. Why is it me?
That's self- talk. Why is this going on? That's self- talk. I can't
leave. That's self- talk. It's the constant mind chatter that is

constantly judging or telling us what or what not to do. The how or how not to do something. The when or when not, or why or the why not to do something. It influences the way we feel and behave.

Have you heard the saying," you can see your glass half full or half empty." The same idea follows with our self- talk. It is our perception. Each and every one of us sees things differently through our own thoughts and beliefs. For example say there is an idea presented by yourself or another person. At first you may think it is a good idea. Through the different thoughts that your mind may bring forward and through this chatter this idea could easily be turned into a bad idea. It can also be influenced by other people's thoughts.

Notice the words you speak when you communicate. Notice if they are empowering you or disempowering you. Are they positive things or negative things you are saying about yourself or others. Use positive affirmations. Surround yourself with people whom are successful and like-minded and are encouraging and open minded and whom want to see you succeed in return. There are also those who care who give honest feedback that is truthful to bring awareness and in turn will help you grow and be your very best. Look yourself in the mirror and speak positive things about yourself. The first time you are talked to negatively you are in shock. The next time someone talks negatively you start getting used to it.

Your environment can influence your self- talk. It doesn't have to be just in the form of words. Our thoughts are created from events or things said through our daily interactions in our surroundings and people we associate with. We judge others and we judge ourselves, our appearance, communication styles, our expectations, the way things are perceived by ourselves and others. We also judge our environment through our experiences with others and the appearance of our surroundings and the sounds we hear. Self- talk is in the mind. Listening to the thoughts that are in your mind. They can propel you or hinder you. Become aware of those thoughts in your mind as awareness of those thoughts will give you an understanding of the results in your daily decisions.

Section 2: Boundaries

There are personal boundaries. There are physical boundaries and sometimes we have emotional boundaries. There are some people who have spiritual boundaries. If we didn't have boundaries we'd be a doormat. We all have boundaries. Our boundaries are usually some of our guidelines of what we allow or don't allow in our lives. Some boundaries we know that we've made or we're aware that we made somewhere we don't acknowledge. For example someone is in a relationship. It's their first love. Their kind of wide open and if they get hurt or they get cheated on or something else we might put a boundary up that we are not going to be vulnerable. We may realize that boundary consciously or we might not.

Boundaries are a huge thing. There are physical boundaries. There are emotional boundaries. Boundaries are guidelines for how we allow people in our lives to treat us or how we allow ourselves to be treated. It is beyond cultural. This is as human beings. In this section we are going to give tools that you can use in your lives that you can look at your own boundaries. Why we choose to stay in a situation that we are at? I'm a caregiver. I've always been a caregiver as a wife in this relationship. I'm supposed to take care of the family. If I leave I can't take care of the family. Another thing that went through my mind was I need to be patient.

Here are some of the reasons why I needed to stay in the situation. My parents were private people they did not discuss our personal matters with everyone nor did my father ask for outside help with my mother. They believed that no matter how difficult times may be we always take care of each other. Sometimes the way that we grow up or our cultures or our perceptions that we are afraid to even talk about it. It doesn't mean we talk about putting it in the local newspaper stand but I mean even to close friends and family. Maybe we stay in the relationship because of legal expenses and complications. My family had never been through a divorce or separation. I didn't even know where to begin or what to do in that regards and I felt so guilty even considering it. I wasn't going to go anywhere near there.

Boundaries are a huge thing of not just how we allow ourselves to be talked to. The reason we need to have boundaries is to protect and take care of ourselves. To be aware of what is good for us or not good for us.

Other boundaries that are important in regards to our self- esteem and in regards to us being confident and fulfilled human beings are confidence, self- control, language, emotional boundaries and physical boundaries.

Part 1: Emotional Boundaries

Someone could say something really nice and if they use a tonality it could be completely degrading. People could say the most horrible thing and say it in a funny tone, and we all start laughing.

Utilize space of your emotional boundary. Our emotions are so strong, and it affects us in so many different areas. Our emotions can affect us mentally; it can affect us spiritually. It can affect us physically. Our emotions can affect us in so many ways.

Are you the type of person that may emotionally over react? Or are you the type of person who just shuts down your emotions, stuffs them down? Neither one is right or wrong. But they both have the price you paid for it. Emotions like anger, sadness, and nervousness are hidden forms of fear. We each react differently when our emotional boundaries get intruded on. Just note how you react.

Sometimes, I would still react the same even though it may be a different situation. And I had to set my emotional boundaries that I wasn't going to react the same out of fear. Or if I went into a different relationship, I wasn't going to be distrusting because my emotional automatic response would kick up. What can I do about it? People don't realize, but we can rationalize our emotions. Too many people let their emotions run them.

Part 2: Physical Boundaries

Physical boundaries are one of the three categories under personal boundaries.

1. Physical: Your body, your house, your desk, your purse, your time, and so forth.
2. Social: The way others treat you, and how you treat others in various social situations.
3. Psychological: Thoughts, beliefs, opinions.

Physical boundaries have to do with space and having your own space. Physical boundaries include respect to the body. Violations include touching someone who does not want to be touched and getting too physically close to someone when interacting with them.

People who go through your things at home or at work violate your physical boundaries. On the website Boundaries for effective Ministry, it says that the Founders of the American Republic thought that personal physical boundaries were so necessary to the pursuit of happiness they enshrined them in the Fourth Amendment to the American Constitution. They said, "The right of people to be secure in their, persons, houses…papers…and effects…shall not be violated…"

Physical boundaries are the lines we draw when it comes to our physical interaction with others. This could be about physically touching someone (a hug, handshake, physical proximity when talking, etc.), but also about the rules we have when spending time with someone (where, when, how long, and what to do, or not do). Deciding how or if we will share our physical body and presence with others.

Our home and surrounding land also represent our physical boundaries. We all have our degree of personal comfort and privacy. Some of us like our curtains drawn; others like them open. Some of us like giving hugs or prefer shaking hands while others have a hard time giving hugs or shaking hands. Lack of physical boundaries can result in violations as a result of crossing the boundary of physical respect and can lead to inappropriate or unwanted touch. It can also create violations as a result of deprivation or not getting enough physical touch as a result one can become an abuser or become depressed.

Physical boundary may mean having a diary that you own. They can be objects that you own. It is your right as a human being to have some things that are yours. It is your right to have a voice of your own.

(a) What would I do if I didn't have physical boundary?

If we don't have physical boundaries with ourselves, we would never stop eating. Or I would never eat. I may not sleep enough. Or I may not exercise enough or over exercise until I am exhausted. Or I may not take care of my physical hygiene and or appearance. Or I may obsess over my appearance and hygiene by not being happy about every aspect of my appearance and clean myself or my surroundings obsessively or compulsively. Without physical boundaries, I would never take time for myself. Or I would give of my time only and not have that balance.

(b) Physical boundaries in relationships

What happens if we don't set our physical boundaries? Then we find ourselves in situations that we don't want to be in. Or I would be so self-absorbed that I would not notice anyone else or hear what another person is sharing with us.

We are constantly giving to others and not so concerned about ourselves. What does that mean that we do? We may neglect ourselves. What is the cost of when we are constantly giving? You are giving away your self-esteem and your self-respect. If we are constantly giving to others and not so concerned about ourselves, what is the cost that we pay? The cost we could pay is our self-respect; the cost we could pay is our self-care. The cost we could pay is our health. The cost we could pay is harbouring resentment. The cost we could pay is rape. We may not want to have sex. But if we don't have physical boundaries, then what? Then we can't say, "I'm really not into this right now." Physical boundaries in relationships may mean that we get hit, and we stay. What does that do? That grants permission for them to hit us again. What is the cost for me? It could be physical abuse.

Part 3: Boundary to voice your own opinion

You have a right to have a voice. To have your own voice is to speak from your authentic self. When we don't speak our opinions, ideas, opportunities, and/or solutions we cannot have a chance to be explored, fulfilled, resolved or heard. A lot of times we do not share our opinions due to fear of acceptance or approval. When we are not heard or able to voice our opinions we withdraw or become angry and resentful. What you can do about it is to speak up and be heard. Believe in what you have to say. Speak through your passion and know that you have a right to be heard. Everyone has a right to their own opinions. Whether you believe in that opinion is an individual choice. Not everyone is right and not everyone is wrong.

Part 4: Boundary of Respect

The boundary of respect is a quality where you feel admiration for someone because of their personal qualities, their achievements, or their status. They show this by treating them in a polite and kind way.

Boundary of respect has a lot to do with our confidence and respecting ourselves and being accepting of who we are is enough. Boundary of respect has a lot to do with self- love.

We not only have the right but the duty to take responsibility of how we allow others to treat us.

The boundary of respect is not always being able to see eye to eye with somebody, but respecting their rights to have their opinions or their beliefs. A boundary of respect would be that it is a living entity a living being. Boundary of respect could mean that life is precious. Respect has great importance in life. If we didn't have boundaries of respect, people would have no legal rights. People would have no health rights. They would have no moral respect. Respecting someone might refer to praising his or her overall as a morally good person, acknowledging that they are equal in the moral community. It's sometimes expressed in turn of a person's right. The boundary of respect for other living human beings is huge.

Respect means not making fun of others. Respect means thinking of how somebody else feels. Respect is treating another person the same way you'd want to be treated. You show respect by just smiling or acknowledging someone. Respect is shown when you are polite by saying please and thank you. You show respect by appreciating people's differences, like seeing someone as unique for the way they dress rather than thinking they are weird for dressing differently. Boundary of respect includes being a good listener even when opinions are different. Lending a hand, showing manners, politeness. Understand if someone expresses fear and is feeling uncomfortable with a situation by not pressuring them further.

Boundary of respect is appreciating things and people for their differences and unique personalities, appearances, likes, and dislikes. This world is full of special people, and we are all deserving of being treated with equal respect.

Section 3: Self-Control

Being in control of self is not being dictated to by someone who tells us what to do and when. I was a very confident young woman as I was quite independent, working, and educating myself at the same time. The next thing I knew I was being controlled. How can you draw your boundary?

- What do we mean by self-control boundaries? Self-control boundaries means that I can control my movement. I am free to go as I want. I could move with ease and by choice.
- How do you set your self-control?

How you can go about saving your own environment is to be able to do a give and take if you are living in a house with somebody then maybe you both decorate the house. It's one thing for a partner to look at you and go I love you in that red dress or please wear the dress or I can't believe your wearing that or I can't believe you went in there. It's important to watch what we are talking about with language.

Confidently Looking Back
and Moving Forward

Life is about persevering and never giving
up in finding out who you truly are.

What is that confidence that you used to have, or I used to have, or I see other people have been through who have survived some of the same circumstances? At one point in my life at the very beginning, I felt like a very confident person. I think we all start off as confident people. It's just we sometimes don't set our boundaries, and our boundaries get blurry. So I want to talk to you about boundaries.

Boundaries allow us the space to maintain our authentic self. Confidence allows us to create and to do what we truly love and to speak freely from our purpose. True confidence comes from our inner strength. It comes from our own achievements. Confidence is also resilience of another. It takes time to build confidence. True confidence doesn't come from the words, we say. It doesn't come necessarily from how we look. Does that help us? Yes. If we look at ourselves and we go wow we look pretty then we could feel more confident. True, confidence comes from our inner strength. It comes from our own achievements or the time that we have had to face adversity and come out the other side. Confidence can delve on you. After a while you can ask yourself wait a minute, "am I the one that's not being right?"

In the Webster's Dictionary, the definition for the word confidence is as follows. "A feeling or consciousness of one's power or the resilience on one's circumstances. Fate or belief that one will ask in an appropriate or affective way. Having confidence as a leader. The quality or state of being. A relation of trust or intimacy. Alliance of a person's expression." Looking at it, there's a part of us that we love the person. We are looking at it, and obviously we could doubt our own confidence if we haven't done anything. If and when we start to doubt the trust or intimacy, if somebody else or somebody we love has a doubt, then we start to wonder about our own decision. We start to doubt our own confidence. Confidence comes from resilience. Confidence comes from achievement.

Once you do something, you become more confident about it. When I spoke on the stage, I was so nervous and even forgot what I was going to say or do. I continued to go back each day to my classes, and the more I did it I was able to finish my speech. Another thing about confidence is when you are looking at other people who survived the same situation and triumphed through it. Not just survived it, but thrived through it. You can also gain confidence by being a mom. You start getting confidence that you can handle the situation. Confidence is also resilience and resilience of another. It takes time to build confidence. Confidence ties into self-esteem and self-trust. Confidence does feel safe in one's self when in one's power without any suggestion of conceit or arrogance. Confidence comes from long experiences. Confidence is speaking up for yourself and for others. It is knowing who you are.

In the Canadian Oxford dictionary confidence means "(1) Firm trust, faith. (2a) self-reliance; belief in one's own abilities (b) assurance or certainty. (3a) Something told confidentially; a secret (shared confidences) (b) the telling of private matters with mutual trust." The meaning of self-confidence in The New Oxford Dictionary of English is "a feeling of trust in one's abilities, qualities, and judgement." When we are living through our authentic self, this is where our true happiness and peace comes from.

Here are a few statistics. I thought I was really alone. What I learned is 1 in 3 women have experienced domestic violence in some point or in some form during their lifetime. I am not the only woman that has gone through this. In ten countries, 55 to 95% of women have never reported any type of mental or physical abuse to government shelters or police if anything. It is well over half of the 1 in 3 out of billions have not reported abuse.

Without help, boys who witness domestic abuse are far more likely to become abusers of their partners and self. Most domestic abuse instances are never reported, whether it is physical or verbal.

Nine out of ten adults' state family abuse or family violence is a much bigger problem than what they know.

Eighty percent of women agree that every woman has something about her that is beautiful, but they do not see their own beauty. Girls are three times more likely than boys to have a negative body image already.

Here are a couple of low self-esteem facts. Low self-esteem is actually a thinking disorder, which an individual views themselves as an inadequate, unworthy, unlovable, or incompetent.

The World Health Organization did worldwide research, and what they discovered for statistics on self-esteem is that in a study 80% of all women complained that their negative body image would link the negative remarks made by friends and family. About 85% of people in the world suffer from low self-esteem, and that some of the consequences and end up being broken relationships, broken relationships with self, and not living up to potential.

Looking back, I definitely would do things differently. But I know if I hadn't have gone through what I've been through then I wouldn't be the same person I am today. In moving forward, I definitely will look for the red flag.

Having gone through what I've gone through and coming out the other side, I've learned it is possible to come out of any situation. It may feel impossible and difficult in the moment, but deal with each situation as it arises and never give up until you see the end result you want to see. Do not settle for less in your heart and in your mind. Keep working through it until you believe you gave it everything you had. Do not give up until you have achieved your end result.

As I am moving forward, this is where I am heading. I look forward to the future. I know what's coming in will be different than the past. As I write this book, I am now a widow as my husband has passed away. He taught me to become more independent, stronger, and to speak up as I had to handle everything, including many obstacles after his passing. He also left me the most precious gift I have received in this lifetime— becoming a mother to a beautiful child. In the very first few months and years of his life, my child's gifts were noticeable. I learned the importance of finding ways to challenge him so he can become the best person he can be. He has taught me so much and has given me so much to look forward to. My vision is to educate him and enrich his life with experiences where he can grow to be someone who is happy and fulfilled within his self, and in turn will give back to society with his talents his passions and help other children and families with a greater vision that this will turn into a domino effect.

My dream is to help other children and families with the similar opportunities the way I have been able to see the growth in my son. I want to give children from low socio-economic backgrounds the funding to receive similar educational opportunities. I recall when I was in high school, there was an exam I had to write and we were marked by percentile. The subject I scored the highest on was the Humanities. I scored above the norm. Now with the personal growth work I have been doing and my freedom of being able to make my own decisions, plus the gift of my son I have learned so much. In moving forward I am continuing to learn my passion of helping on a greater level has never been stronger. I can see my authentic self. I know as time passes by, my vision will become clearer as I move forward on my own personal growth and journey. My intention for my future is one with inner peace and abundance in all areas of my life. I knew from the time I was very young I had a higher calling. I knew all the hurdles and struggles and experiences were there for me for a bigger purpose. I was meant to do and experience all those things that were there on my path. One of my greatest challenges in my life was learning to trust people. I am a highly sensitive person, and there was a time I became emotional very easily by the way people communicated to me or in my presence of others. My education and numerous experiences working with people and interacting with them has helped and moulded me to who I am today. Through my own personal growth journey, I have learned that our outer world is the mirror of our inner world, and it is up to us to take the responsibility to reflect what we want to see by changing our thoughts. I learned that we need to be the change before we can see the change we want to see in our world. I have always been on the quest of personal growth. I have always had a passion and love for helping people. One of the things that give me the greatest pleasure is to acknowledge and cheer another person when they are in my presence.

Moving forward I know for me after everything I've been through, it's not always easy to trust. I've decided that I'm not just going to wall myself up to never trust because if you don't trust, you can't love. I don't know about you, but I'm sure it's not going to be easy for you to trust either if you've been in a situation like mine. This is why we want to trust. I believe trust is built from respect. Lack of trust kicks in for me when the respect is broken. I believe respect is vital and huge when it comes to trust.

From the time I was young, some of my greatest supporters and teachers have been my parents, particularly my mother who was blind, as well as those people with special needs and the elderly people I have had the privilege of caring for over the years. Their unconditional love and support will never be forgotten. They never criticised or judged me and were always there throughout the years. Some were verbal and others nonverbal. I understood that the behaviors and actions and words of certain people were the result of their illness and not the person. I am at a place where I am so hopeful, and I feel so blessed and privileged that I have had the privilege from learning from amazing leaders and human potential leaders whom I have studied with, and some whom I have personally met. One of whom I so gratefully feel honoured of working with on this book with is Shellie Hunt. She has been mentoring and coaching me through this journey I am headed on with my writing. I never imagined that I could and would be able to write a book for adults. I just thought it would be children's books that I would write until I met our beautiful, inspiring, and amazing Shellie Hunt who saw a lot more than I did in myself. There are no words to describe the gratitude of knowing that someone who firstly, did not know me from a hole in the ground was willing to work with me. She is a compassionate humanitarian leader and is someone who is recognized amongst world leaders and was willing to take me on and work with me. I never imagined that someone of her caliber would be willing to work with me. I have always hoped and dreamt of learning from the best, and now I have the opportunity to work with and learn from the best.

I believe I have found my authentic self as I love to learn and be challenged with the greater intention of helping mankind. If you are someone who is reading, then I know you can too.

Safety

"It is only when your inner world feels safe that
your outer world will feel like a safer place as well.
The change must come from within you first."

What is safety? Safety is to protect oneself from being harmed and keeping those around us safe from harm as well. How do you make a change and safely make the change? Become aware of your thoughts and feelings. Be conscious of your physical safety and boundaries if needed. Get protection by seeking help from an outside source. You must want to make the change and make it your choice.

When in a relationship or when communicating with someone, have you expressed what you don't like in that person? It could be their behavior or actions that you don't like. If you feel that the person is not hearing you then you need to assess how you are feeling around that behavior. If you are feeling unhappy, anxious, fear, unable to communicate, feeling that you are having difficulty trusting and maybe even feeling threatened for your safety, it is best to reach out to someone you may feel safe with and remove yourself from the situation so you can assess your thoughts. Sometimes it is best to communicate with an outside source as in a counselor, a friend, or family member so you can express and have someone to just listen to you. Sometimes communicating with another person helps you find the clarity you need to become clear with your feelings and the situation to be able to really see what you need to do for yourself.

Really assess what it is you want for yourself. Ask yourself questions. How do you want to feel? What do you need to do to feel that way? What kinds of things do you need to do to make those changes? What kinds of people do you need to surround yourself with to make those changes? How are you helping the other person if they are not hearing what you have to say, and all you can feel is fear, anxiety, anger, etc.?

The most important person to take care of is you. If you can't help yourself, you cannot help another person. In order for someone to change, they first have to be aware that there is a problem. Second, they need to want to change that feeling or behavior. You need to become aware of your thoughts, your feelings, your actions, and behaviors. When you get to the place of anger of that is enough and that you cannot take anymore, that is when change can take place.

Visualize what it is you want and take the actions that will lead you to what you want. For example surround yourself with people who are warm, caring, great listeners, and treat you with respect. Do not give into anything less than what you want. Observe the way people communicate. How do they treat you and others around them? Watch their actions. Do they follow through with what they say? Do you feel comfortable and safe when around them? To trust takes time. It takes time to get to know people. First impression is not always a reliable way to judge someone.

As one grows, one changes. By becoming aware of what you can change to feel happier and safer you now have the insight that when we feel that uncomfortable feeling we can take different action. As we change, people around us may become angry, become fearful, may even be threatening because they may be scared because they don't know what to expect. They fear they are losing you. You always need to maintain your safety and remember what your goal is for yourself no matter how kind one may become. Remember the patterns. Change cannot happen without action, perseverance, determination, commitment, accountability, decision, and personal choice. One needs to change for themselves, not for another person or because of another person. That type of change will be temporary or not existent.

This is Your Family, and This Is an Important Message

Life is a journey of experiences that are there to
lead you to your greater purpose in this world.

Accept yourself and others the way you and they are. No one is perfect. Learn from whatever you fear. Everyone comes into our lives for a reason, and everything in life happens for a reason. It is a matter of taking that what happens or those we meet and use that information as a growing experience. It happened to us to learn from and grow from. Everything and everyone has a message for us. Be aware of your strengths and weaknesses. Take your weaknesses and create them into your strengths, and they can lead you to your purpose. Look at your strengths, and they can lead you to your passions. It is through the pain and fear that we grow and become stronger. Remember, no one is less than anyone else. We are all connected. We all are on this planet because we all have a gift or gifts.

You are important on the face of this planet because you have a role to play. And you are meant to be here because you are here to learn and grow and to teach others. You are important because every single person on this planet is here and is serving a purpose, and each and every one of you has a role to play in making a change through your presence in the way you impact the people you meet and the world at large. It is through your presence and your talents, your smile, your heart, your appearance, your words, your actions, your love, your emotions, your uniqueness, and your experiences. It is only through you that you can impact the lives of others and as a result the planet as a whole. We all have a purpose because of our role. The more we become aware through our choices, the more we can make more conscious decisions not only for ourselves but all those and everything we impact around us. Just know you are stronger than you know. Do you remember being authentic as a child? You are authentically yourself.

15

Tools

Self-Esteem Enrichment Builders

"Anything can be overcome it is finding
and implementing the right tools, resources
and support system that will work for
you and get you to the next level."

People need self- esteem survival all the time. We need it
when someone breaks up with us. We need it when we
break up with someone. We need it when we get divorced.
We need it when a family member relative or friend dies.
We need it when we have a horrible job, and we have just
been stuck in it. We need it when we may be going through
a down period in our lives, and we need something to lift

ourselves up. Or our boss is horrible or unfair to us or the environment we work in is not in our purpose or is a negative place to be. Or maybe we are just dedicating our whole life to our children, which is wonderful; however, we don't give to ourselves. Then we get lost in that. Our kids grow up and they go to school and then get married, and then we wonder how come we don't have a life.

The enrichment builders are ideas that can help us feel good about ourselves and the world around us. The key is to use them. I know from experience they work. Some of these ideas will help you connect to what you are seeking through your own inner awareness. Some can be fun, educational, and may even help you grow by trying something new. If you feel something does not work for you, try something different. You can even make it a game and do different variations of the ideas listed.

Here are some ideas for you to use:

- Physically working out.
- Have your hair done.
- Have a girlfriend do your hair.
- Trying a new hair design.
- Going to a children's hospital and helping them.
- Going out with your girlfriend.
- Watching a funny show or movie.
- Sometimes it's as simple as submitting an article in your local newspaper as people see themselves in there.

- Manicure.
- How about doing something you have never done and try it? Like I am going to go horseback riding and actually go one day.
- Going to a place of worship.
- Serving your community.
- Pedicure.
- Go to a makeup outlet like Sears, Mac, The Bay, Macy's where you can have your makeup done for you where they can do your face if you are someone who wears makeup or if you would like to try make up on for the first time.
- Buy a new hairdo.
- Buy a new outfit.
- Read a daily quote from Louise Hay every day.
- Find something to hang on your wall at home or office wall that is a positive trigger device for you every day.
- Martial Arts.
- Yoga class.
- Take lessons to learn to play an instrument of your choice.
- Attend a fitness class.
- Go to a community centre and take a class of your liking like art, pottery, and dance.
- Try different clothes on and have a picture taken of you in those outfits.

- Decorate your home or have someone help decorate it.
- Rearrange your furniture.
- Gather things you own that you no longer need and have a garage sale.
- Go for a walk around your neighbourhood.
- Tutor someone in a subject that you love to teach.
- Sit out in nature and let go of all thoughts in your mind and focus on the present moment.
- Clear your mind of all thoughts and focus on the word love.
- Go for a run or jog.
- Spa treatment.
- Go to a movie by yourself or with someone else.
- Work in a garden.
- Plant vegetables and/or flowers.
- Buy indoor plants and care for them by watering them regularly and watching them grow.
- Take a Toastmasters course or Dale Carnegie course in public speaking and human relations.
- Find a mentor/coach to do personal development work with.
- Take the Millionaire Mind Intensive through Peak Potentials or take any Peak Potential course.
- Become a member of CEO Space.
- Listen to audio or read books on topics you love.
- Read books like Napoleon Hill, *Secret*, Personal development books, Joe Vitale, John Assaraf, Louise

Hay, Bob Proctor, *Supreme Influence* by Nuirka. Learn from their teachings.

- Watch Guy Finley on Youtube.
- Do volunteer work for your church.
- Volunteer for your community.
- Volunteer in a hospital, Long term care ward, or in an old Age home.
- Help people with special needs.
- Take kickboxing class.
- Have an animal or pet to care for and play with like a cat, dog, bird, or fish.
- Watch comedy shows.
- Be around funny people.
- Laugh
- Smile when communicating.
- Consciously be aware of speaking positively about yourself.
- Say positive things about yourself as you look in the mirror. Tell yourself all the things you love about yourself.
- Sit by water (waterfall, ocean, lake, river, pond) and be present with the sounds and the scenery around you and the things you can touch.
- Read comic strips.
- Read funny books and stories.
- Sing your favorite songs.
- Sing karaoke with your friends or by yourself.

- Write your thoughts on paper whatever is on your mind.
- Create a vision board of all the things you would love to have in your life by cutting out pictures and words from magazines.
- Go for a hike.
- Do some arts and crafts.
- Sew, knit, and crochet.
- Visit some friends.
- Learn something new that you have always wanted to learn to do.
- Visit a place that you really love or have always wanted to see.
- Take a cruise.
- Travel by train or plane to a destination of your choice.
- Go for a drive.
- Help an elderly person in your neighborhood with their garden or something they may need help with.
- Play with a child or children. Play a board game or play sports with them.
- Do a crossword puzzle.
- Do word searches.
- Do a jigsaw puzzle.
- Create your own cards, jewelry, candles, soaps, chocolates.
- Join a craft fair and sell your creations or baking.
- Dress up and look your best.

- If you won an award, hang it on the wall.
- Recognize, celebrate and appreciate your accomplishments and list them on paper and read them out loud.
- When you wake up in the morning start your day by saying "I love my life," and "This is going to be an amazing day." It will start your day with an energizing boost.
- Listen to OmHarmonics.
- Do meditations.
- Learn from Master Trivedi and experience the Trivedi Effect.
- Listen to Sonia Ricotti, Anthony Roberts, Paul Scheele, paraliminals
- Watch and listen to Mind Movies Matrix.
- Read stories to your children.
- Bake or cook your favorite dish and share your food with people you love or whom would appreciate the food. Or you can share with those at work.
- Volunteer at an outreach program and prepare sandwiches and drinks for those in need.
- Donate blood to the Red Cross.

Resources

http://www.rescue.org/womenandgirls

http://www.nationalhomeless.org/factsheets/domestic.html

National Coalition Against Domestic Violence, P.O. Box 18749, Denver, CO, 80218-0749; 303/839-1852, Fax: 303/831-9251.

National Coalition for the Homeless, 2201 P St NW, Washington, DC 20037, 202.462.4822

National Domestic Violence Hotline, 3616 Far West Boulevard, Suite 101 297, Austin, TX 78731-3074. Hotline numbers: 1-800-799-SAFE(7233), 1-800-787-3224 (TDD).

National Resource Center on Domestic Violence, 6400 Flank Dr., Suite 1300, Harrisburg, PA 17112-2778; 800/537-2238.

National Clearinghouse for the Defense of Battered Women, 125 S. 9th St., Suite 302,

Philadelphia, PA 19107-5116; 215/351-0010; Fax: 215/351-0779.

http://www.thehotline.org/

http://www.helpguide.org/mental/domestic_violence_abuse _help_treatment_prevention.htm

http://www.hotpeachpages.net/ International Directory of Domestic Violence Agencies

http://www.rainn.org/get-help/sexual-assault-and-rape-international-resources

http://dahmw.org/

http://www.nationaldomesticviolencehelpline.org.uk/

http://refuge.org.uk/about-us/what-we-do/helpline/

http://www.bwss.org/

http://www.familyservicetoronto.org/programs/vaw/centres. html

http://866uswomen.org/

http://www.angelscommunity.com/EN/crisis_lines/

http://www.rapereliefshelter.BC.ca/help/escape-abusive-man/ escape-abusive-man

http://www.wrsfv.ca/programs/transition_house/transition_ houses.html

http://www.rapereliefshelter.BC.ca/sites/default/files/imce/ Blue_Pamphlet.pdf

http://www.lfcc.on.ca/ralinks.html

http://www.povnet.org/find-an-advocate/BC/crisis-services
http://www.bcsth.ca/content/other-resources-0
http://www.povnet.org/node/3493
http://www.bcwomens.ca/Services/HealthServices/Woman
AbuseResponse/FindHelp.htm